First published in Great Britain 2021 by 100% Unofficial,
a part of Farshore

An imprint of HarperCollins*Publishers*
1 London Bridge Street, London SE1 9GF
www.farshore.co.uk

HarperCollins*Publishers*
1st Floor, Watermarque Building, Ringsend Road
Dublin 4, Ireland

Written by Daniel Lipscombe
Edited by Craig Jelley
Designed by Ian Pollard
Illustrations by Matt Burgess
Cover designed by John Stuckey
Cover illustrations by Ryan Marsh

ISBN 978 0 7555 0108 3
Printed in Romania
001

ONLINE SAFETY FOR YOUNGER FANS

Spending time online is great fun! Here are a few simple rules to help younger fans stay safe and keep the internet a great place to spend time.

- Never give out your real name – don't use it as your username.
- Never give out any of your personal details.
- Never tell anybody which school you go to or how old you are.
- Never tell anybody your password, except a parent or guardian.
- Be aware that you must be 13 or over to create an account on many sites. Always check the site policy and ask a parent or guardian for permission before registering.
- Always tell a parent or guardian if something is worrying you.

Stay safe online. Any website addresses listed in this book are correct at the time of going to print. However, Farshore is not responsible for content hosted by third parties. Please be aware that online content can be subject to change and websites can contain content that is unsuitable for children. We advise that all children are supervised when using the internet.

100% UNOFFICIAL

ROBLOX ANNUAL 2022

CONTENTS

HELLO READERS!

Welcome back to the many worlds of Roblox!

With so many places to go and games to play, there's never a dull moment for Robloxians. Every time you click play, you're opening a portal to a new world and experience. This year, there are lots of games to talk about and show off. Everything from job simulators, to popular obbys and pets galore.

Join us as we rediscover what makes Roblox so unique. Hopefully you'll see some games you love and a few future faves. There are quizzes and puzzles, plenty of laughs and lots more beyond that.

All of the biggest games are here; we'll check in with Adopt Me!, Bloxburg and Royale High. Together, we'll hide from menacing players, look into which games are hidden gems, apply for the best jobs and learn to duck and dive around the awesome obbys.

Grab your controller, tablet or boot up your PC and log in; we've got so much to cover! Don't forget to message your friends, get them online and ...

Let's start playing!

A YEAR IN ROBLOX

It's been yet another jam-packed year for Roblox, one in which an increasing number of people have turned to online platforms to interact and socialise with their buddies. Here's a rundown of the headlines from a year in Roblox.

3 BILLION HOURS

During the past year, over 3 BILLION hours of play was logged with Roblox. To put that massive number into perspective, it's the equivalent of over 342,000 years of play time!

150 MILLION PLAYERS

It's not much of a surprise that players reached that many hours when Roblox now has over 150 million active players. Think of all those people across the world playing together!

PLAYING THROUGH THE PANDEMIC

Of course, 2020 saw the world become socially distant due to the coronavirus pandemic. Players swamped the Roblox servers in order to spend time with friends they couldn't see in real life. Some smart devs launched Party Place, an area for players to host birthday parties while in lockdown.

LEARNING

As they do every year, Roblox hosted competitions for kids to learn how to code games using their simple tools. Not only were kids learning to code, but they also had reminders on how to behave online, spot fake news and stay safe online through videos and online scavenger hunts.

PLAY TOGETHER

Due to the need for people to connect more, Roblox launched private servers, where players could gather with their friends in peace. The system became available for everyone and it really helped people stay connected. Why not see if your favourite game has private servers?

THE 2021 BLOXY AWARDS

In March 2021, thousands of people gathered online for the 8th Annual Bloxy Awards, which gave out prizes for the best games on Roblox. Did your favourite earn an award?

GAME OF THE YEAR Piggy	**SLEEPER HIT** Super Doomspire	**BEST GAME TRAILER** Tower Defense Simulator
AWARD OF EXCELLENCE Piggy	**MOBILE GAME OF THE YEAR** Super Golf!	**XBOX GAME OF THE YEAR** Phantom Forces
BEST NEW GAME Brookhaven	**MOST EDUCATIONAL GAME** Lua Learning	**BEST LIVE EVENT** RB Battles

THE BIG CITY

Bustling with people and chock-full of things to do, big city sims are popular destinations for Robloxians. Whether you're interested in working towards your dream job, raising a family, or just exploring a whole new metropolis, these city games have got you covered.

WELCOME TO BLOXBURG

Bloxburg seems like a great place to live. There's a bit of everything: lots of friendly people, jobs to make some cash and minigames to pass your free time. You can raise a family, cruise around in a car, or decorate your house to make it feel like a home. Whatever you choose to do, Bloxburg more than welcomes it.

FUN FACT

It's not all about working and shopping, you'll need to care for your avatar too, making sure they've got enough food and are fully entertained.

FUN FACT

Since release in 2016, Welcome to Bloxburg has had over TWO BILLION visits, making it one of the most popular games.

Choosing a career is an important decision – everyone needs a job, so there are lots to go round; from fisherman to hairdresser. All of them will reward you with cash for shopping sprees.

You can even build a house from scratch in Bloxburg, choosing all the fixtures and fittings. The only limit to building is your imagination. Have you always wanted a library? Home cinema? These can all be yours … once you've got the money of course!

BROOKHAVEN RP

Brookhaven is home to what some call 'proper role-play'. It's full of players who log in to live out their dream life – some like to be parents and raise children, where the kids go to school while the grown-ups are at work. They drive around on weekends, shopping in local stores and hanging out with friends.

FUN FACT

When buying a vacant lot for your house, you can choose from several great styles for free.

Of course, some visit Brookhaven to simply explore. Hopping in a car, you can drive around and see the sights. Hop out and swap into a faster car or just head home and do some upgrades to your house.

FUN FACT

Some people in role-playing games really commit to their characters, which can lead to fun encounters. How will you react to the residents of Brookhaven?

Brookhaven is full of tiny details, from diners to places of worship. Whatever you want in your digital life, it's possible to experience it with over 60,000 other players.

ALSO TRY

MEEPCITY

EMERGENCY RESPONSE: LIBERTY COUNTY

GREENVILLE

CITY WALK

Can you find your way through the busy city streets?

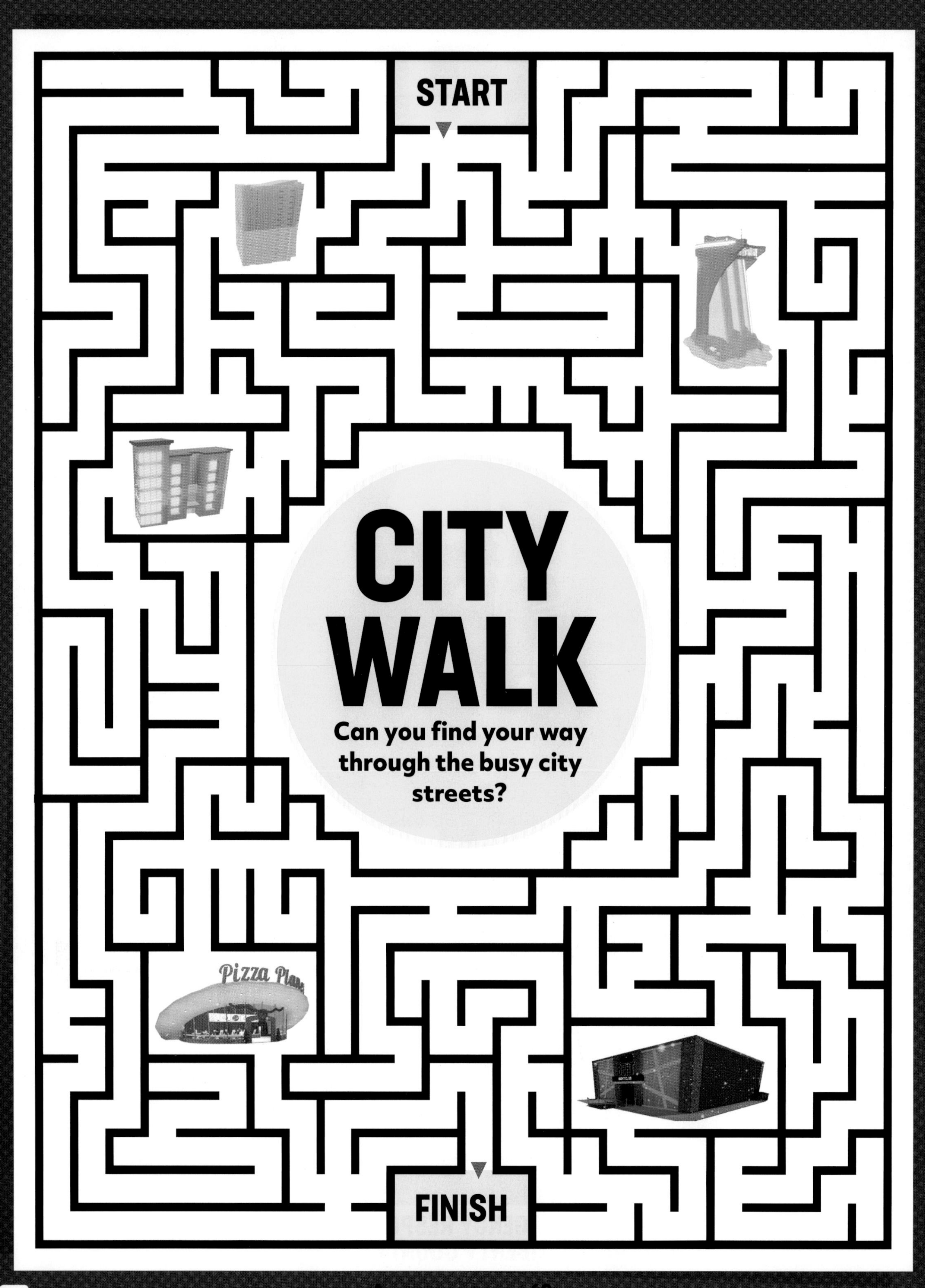

Answers on page 69

MEEPCITY SUDOKU

Use your sudoku skills to solve these puzzles! There can only be one of each colour meep in every row, column and box.

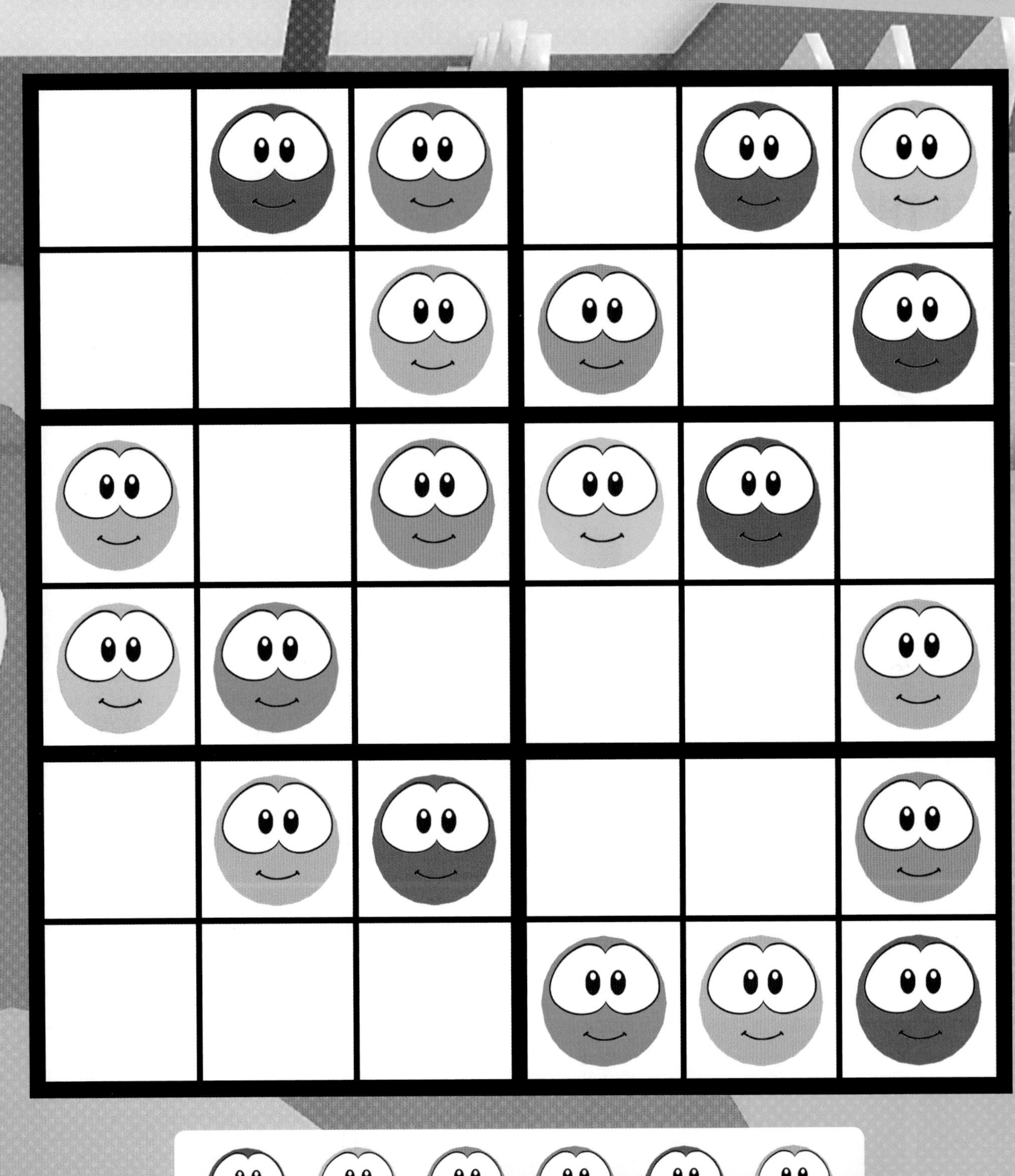

RED ORANGE GREEN BLUE PURPLE GREY

Answers on page 69

SURVIVAL

Sometimes escape isn't an option. Sometimes, you just need to survive. Danger comes in many forms, from killer sharks (or humans ...), to natural disasters and escaped creatures. All you need to do is run, hide and stay alive, which might be easier said than done ...

FLEE THE FACILITY

A monster has escaped! One player takes the role of the monster while four others become survivors. It's up to the survivors to avoid the monster and hack computers to open the exit.

Hacking takes time and when that monster is creeping around, the tension is unbearable! To win, survivors must make it out the exit, while the monster must devour them all!

SURVIVE THE KILLER

In this game, the killer looks just like everyone else and hides in plain sight. As the killer, it's your job to eliminate all the other players. As a survivor, you have to avoid being caught and escape to safery when the exits open. Survive the Killer offers a fun multiplayer experience with tense set pieces, clever hiding places and heart-racing action sequences.

SHARKBITE

A peaceful day on the lake turns deadly when someone lets a monstrous shark into the water. The predator is being controlled by a player and it's up to you to survive on a boat, or bravely take on the shark and eliminate it. As the shark, you'll be busy trying to nom down anyone you spot in the water or destroy boats of potential hunters.

NATURAL DISASTER SURVIVAL

You never quite know what to expect in this game. Hunker down and stay safe because as soon as the disaster begins, things get dangerous really fast. It might be a sandstorm blowing buildings apart, or an earthquake throwing everyone around. The idea is simple: avoid danger and survive for as long as you can.

HIDDEN GEMS

It's always nice to find a game which is slowly building up its playerbase. It's great to be the one showing off a new game to your friends. We've dug into the depths of Roblox to find a couple of games that are shimmering just under the surface.

COLOUR RUSH

A great party game for a huge group of people, Colour Rush is a mad dash to be crowned the fastest thinker. Players enter an arena made up of coloured squares. When a colour is announced, players rush to stand on a square of that colour. If you can't find the correct colour to stand on, you'll fall through the floor and lose a life. Lose two lives and you're out! The last one standing is crowned the winner in a battle-royale style system.

WAYFORT BETA

The Wayfort Beta is a great driving game, where you earn money in order to buy even better cars. It looks stunning and all the cars are modelled as closely as possible to their real-life counterparts. Each one handles very differently, making this more of a simulator than an arcade racer. Other players are roaming about ready to race, whether through the winding streets or out at the drag strip.

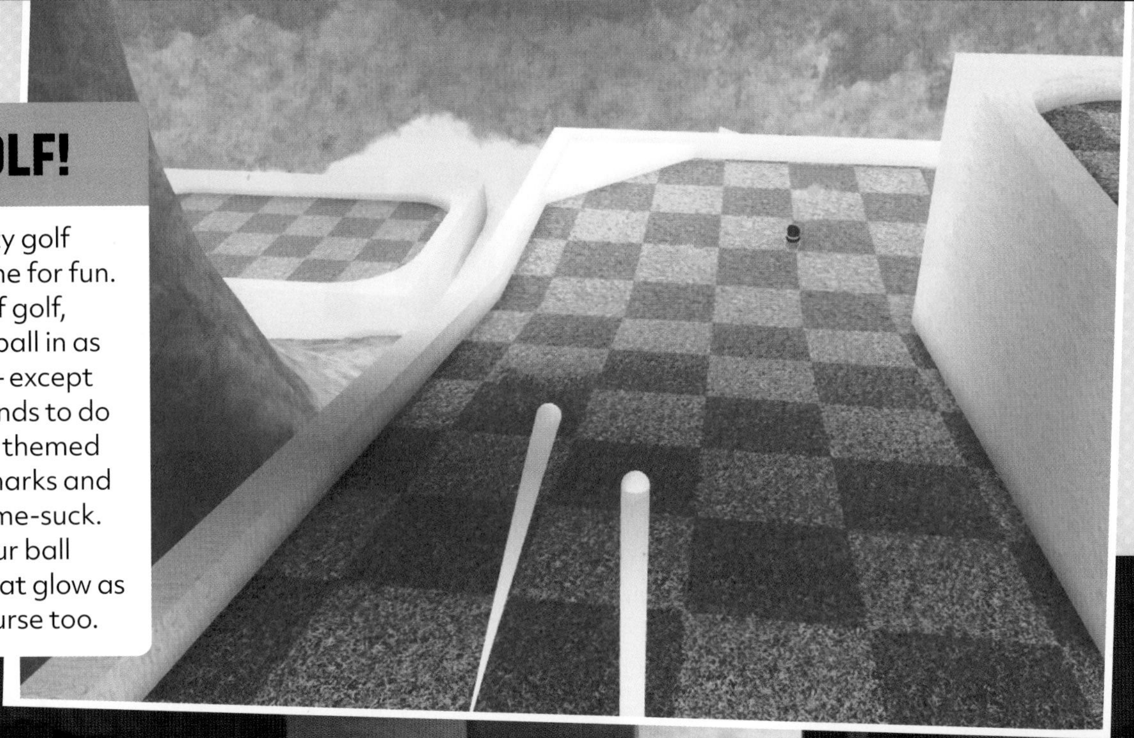

SUPER GOLF!

This arcade-style crazy golf game gets a hole in one for fun. Like a normal round of golf, you've got to sink the ball in as few shots as possible – except you only have 60 seconds to do it! Add in cool courses themed around famous landmarks and you've got a frantic time-suck. You can customise your ball with hats and trails that glow as it rolls through the course too.

SPIDER

If you don't like spiders, it's probably best to give this a miss, because being chased a by a human-sized spider will give you nightmares. This is a great game designed to make players work together in order to escape from the mutant spider and solve the mystery of its origins.

You can only carry one item at a time, which makes it even scarier, as you run around and explore, never knowing if you'll turn a corner and see eight eyes staring back at you ...

PERFECT PETS

If there's one universal love that Robloxians share, it's pets. Whether you're a fan of cats or more of a dog person, everyone has a kindred animal that they would like to adventure with. Roblox has plenty of games that allow you to do just that!

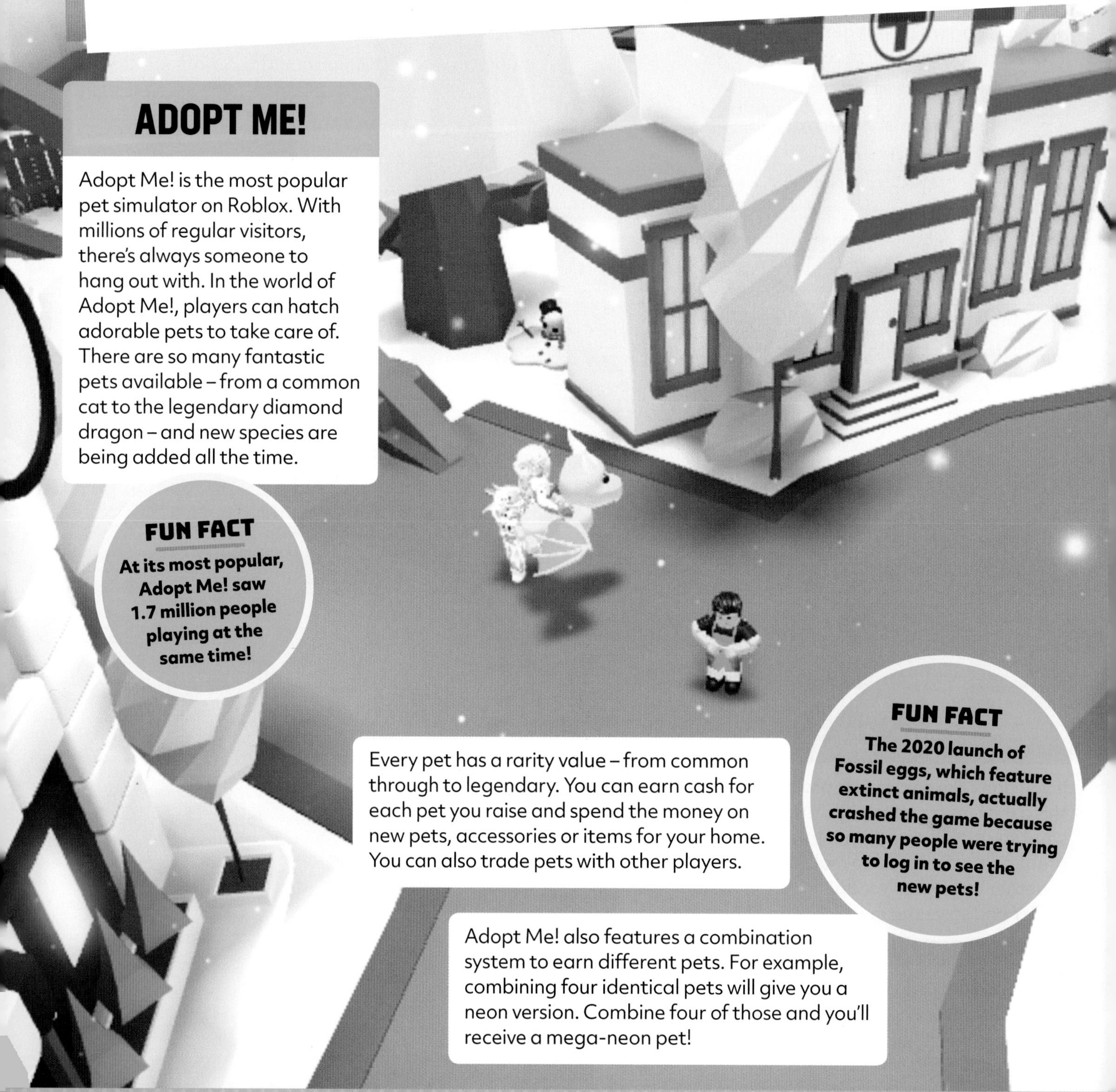

ADOPT ME!

Adopt Me! is the most popular pet simulator on Roblox. With millions of regular visitors, there's always someone to hang out with. In the world of Adopt Me!, players can hatch adorable pets to take care of. There are so many fantastic pets available – from a common cat to the legendary diamond dragon – and new species are being added all the time.

FUN FACT

At its most popular, Adopt Me! saw 1.7 million people playing at the same time!

Every pet has a rarity value – from common through to legendary. You can earn cash for each pet you raise and spend the money on new pets, accessories or items for your home. You can also trade pets with other players.

FUN FACT

The 2020 launch of Fossil eggs, which feature extinct animals, actually crashed the game because so many people were trying to log in to see the new pets!

Adopt Me! also features a combination system to earn different pets. For example, combining four identical pets will give you a neon version. Combine four of those and you'll receive a mega-neon pet!

PET BATTLE SIMULATOR

This is a 'clicker' game, where you recruit pets to fight huge monsters. Starting with a small common pet, players click a button to attack the enemy in an arena. If your fingers get tired, you can unlock 'auto-click' to automate the process.

FUN FACT

The rarest pet is the HUGE Dominus – there's only a tiny chance to hatch this pet. The odds are 1 in TWO MILLION.

Pets come in all shapes and sizes – deer, bears, buckets and spades – yes, you read that right – and seasonal pets like the halloween Jack-O-Lantern! By fighting, players earn gems and sweets which can be traded for eggs to hatch new fighters.

FUN FACT

There are plenty of buffs to apply to your pets when you complete tasks or discover secrets. These can range from double damage in battles to extra gems as rewards.

Players can only equip up to six pets at once, so choose carefully to rack up big damage. Every pet has different stats, so you'll often see other players with entirely different teams. You can train your pets to fight harder, complete quests and explore several islands, all of which have unique pets to hatch.

ALSO TRY

ANIMAL SIMULATOR

TAPPING LEGENDS

PET SIMULATOR

ANIMAL JUMBLES

Can you rearrange these anagrams to find the names of some interesting pets?

Answers on page 69

PET PAIRS

Follow the line through the jumble from each pet to find their favourite item.

Answers on page 69

BEST ROBLOX JOBS

Entire games can be built around one small job in Roblox, like delivering pizzas! But the best games give you the chance to experience roles and jobs that you always want to try in the real world. Let's take a look at some of the most interesting!

OUTLAW

THE WILD WEST

Okay, so outlaw isn't a 'job' really, but people certainly make money from it, and it's rootin' tootin' fun! When entering The Wild West, you can band together with other players to pull off heists or hunt wildlife. As long as you stay away from the law, everything you find is yours to keep. With an arsenal of guns to sling, nobody's loot is safe, and if you can't find a weapon, there's always a chance for a fist fight instead!

NINJA

SHADOWSTORM: NINJA LEGENDS

If someone asked you what you wanted to do for a living and you found out that ninjas got paid for quests, you'd probably choose it, right? They have a great uniform, are as silent as mice and are always wearing slippers – plus they get to wield awesome swords and katanas! That's exactly what you can do in this game too!

FARMER

ISLANDS

It's one of the oldest jobs in the world and there's nothing more calming than farming. Except maybe sleeping. In Islands, you'll sow seeds, harvest crops, chop trees and pull up grass. But the best bit? Building things from the materials you gather. From rudimentary tools to large items of furniture and even monumental buildings, you'll never run out of things to do on your own private island.

GHOSTHUNTER

PARANORMICA

What does every ghosthunter have in their backpack? Salt and crucifixes to scare away ghosts and demons, of course. And you'll need a torch for when things get spooky, and a video camera to record it all. With your paranormal paraphenalia packed, you're ready to go. But it's not a job for the faint of heart – you'll be exploring lots of dark, creepy houses trying to find, talk to and capture spirits!

LUMBERJACK

LUMBER TYCOON 2

Being a lumberjack starts off fairly easy, by selling random logs at the local warehouse. But after a few trips, players have enough money for a small axe, to make chopping and clearing trees easier. This builds steadily, wood sells for a good price and suddenly the money is rolling in! At this point, a lumberjack can buy their own land, install a sawmill and get vehicles to transport wood as their empire begins to grow ...

CHOOSING THE BEST GAMES

There are so many games on Roblox that it can be tough to figure out which one is right for you. Perhaps you live for adrenaline, or maybe you prefer something a bit more chill. There's something for everyone on Roblox, it's just a case of knowing where to look.

CATEGORIES

When you first land on the Games page of Roblox, you'll see rows of colourful title cards for games, broken down into categories, themes or popularity. Whether you're a new player or have been around for ages, it's worth knowing what kind of games you can find in each one.

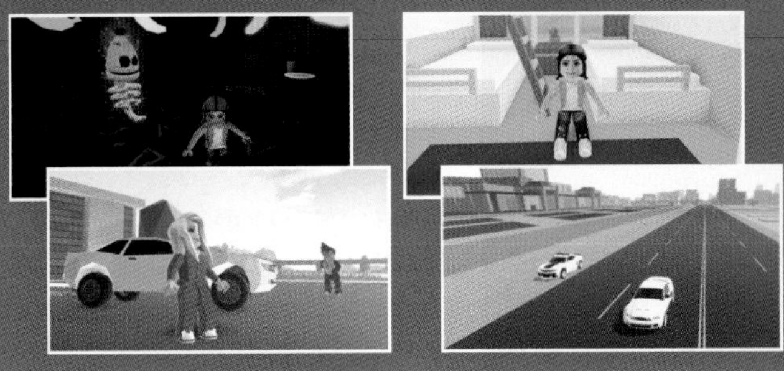

MOST ENGAGING

These are games which keep players coming back time and again. They're the ones that people have spent the most time playing.

RECOMMENDED FOR YOU

This row of games is curated just for you, and features recommendations based on what you've been playing already.

UP-AND-COMING

Games under this heading are those that are starting to gain some traction, get more players and could be the next big thing.

POPULAR

This one is kind of obvious ... They're the games that everyone is playing. This is based purely on the number of visits rather than play time.

TOP RATED

These games are the ones that have made the best impression on players and gained the highest average score of their peers.

LEARN AND EXPLORE

The games here can be educational or will teach you something as you play. They can range from simple maths games to coding lessons.

FEATURED

The featured track has games that have been specially selected by the Roblox team – they normally have some unique innovation.

RTHRO

Every game in the Rthro tag has been optimised for the newest style of avatar and make use of the more human-like proportions in-game.

ROLE-PLAY

A role-play game tasks the player with taking on a role within a world; you might be a cop, a robber, a paramedic, firefighter or maybe even a chef.

ADVENTURE

Fancy some excitement? The adventure tag has you covered; these games will require more skill and feature lots more action than others.

FIGHTING

Whether you love martial arts fist fights or just a frantic first-person shooter, the fighting category has got what you need.

OBBY

Short for obstacle course – not like you'd find in a local playground though. These courses feature fire, spikes or endless mazes to navigate!

TYCOON

Want to manage a tropical resort? Or maybe a theme park? This is where you'll find places to make your dreams comes true.

SIMULATOR

A bit like role-play, the simulator category asks you to take on a role, though the tasks are usually more active and have elaborate rewards.

GAME PAGE

Once you've found a game to play, you'll open the game page. Of course, we expect you'll excitedly press the big 'play button' first of all. Go for it! But when you come back out, there are some bits of interesting info that you can source from the launch page.

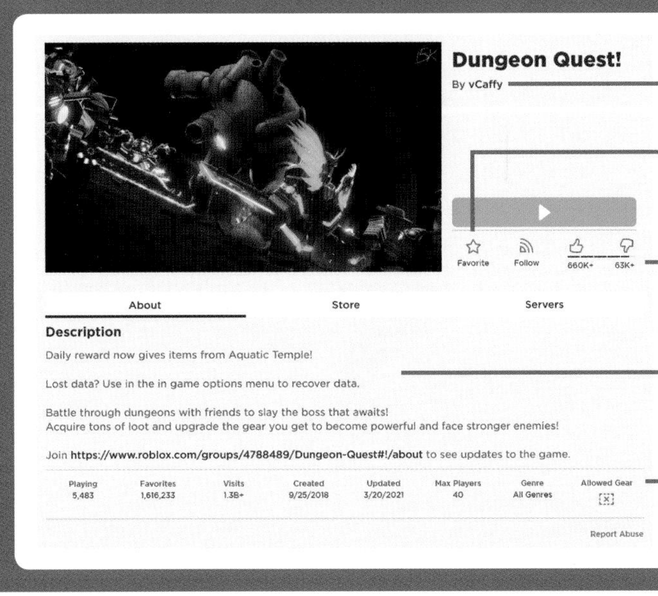

DEVELOPER If you like a game, you can click through to see if the dev has made any others.

FAVOURITE Add this to your list of favourite games so you can easily access it again.

RATINGS Let the community know what you think of a game with a thumbs-up or -down.

DESCRIPTION Find out more details about the game before you jump in.

STATS Discover how many times a game has been played, favourited, and other info.

PLAYING ROLES

Sometimes what you need is an escape from real life; a chance to be someone completely different. Whether you want to become a fluttering fairy or flip dough in a pizza paradise, you can find a new life in this pair of popular games.

ROYALE HIGH

Even if you're still in school, Royale High is a great place to hang out with friends. Probably because it's so different to normal school – for a start, everyone's a fairy. Oh and you also earn diamonds for attendance ...

FUN FACT

There are lots of different lessons to take at Royale High, including swimming, baking, art and chemistry.

Using diamonds, players can change the look of their fairy student from a collection of hundreds of different accessories, clothes and make-up options. It's a true role-playing game, where you can act out any magical high school dream.

FUN FACT

As you play, you will earn badges for certain in-game actions and achievements. There's even one for playing with an influencer!

The better grades you get, the more experience you earn to level up your fairy. You have to make sure you get to class on time and bring the correct books! School isn't just lessons – there are lots of mini-games to play and areas to explore to break up your day!

WORK AT A PIZZA PLACE

Who knew working at a pizza place could be so much fun? You get to choose from several jobs; operating the tills, making pizzas, or delivering to houses in the town.

Residents will order food in-store and from their homes, and you have to do your best to deliver the freshest, tastiest experience with your team. If you don't cook the pizza fast enough, there's nothing to box up and deliver, resulting in a sad customer.

FUN FACT

One of the most popular job simulators, Work at a Pizza Place has been around for TEN YEARS and it still sees thousands of new players every day.

FUN FACT

It's not all about pizza. With the money you earn from working, you can upgrade and decorate your house nearby. You need somewhere to relax when not at work, after all.

Maybe you and your pals will head to party island after work – a place where you can dance and unwind from your day job. We like the sound of that – you'll bring the pizza, of course ...

ALSO TRY

CLUB ROBLOX

ANOMIC

OVERLOOK BAY

★ GENRE DEEP-DIVE ★

SCARY GAMES

It's good to challenge your mind occasionally, and Roblox is home to plenty of scares. Whether you want to play as a monster or run away from one, maybe even fight it head-on, there's a game on the platform for you ... you don't even need to wait for Halloween!

PIGGY

Piggy is THE horror game taking Roblox by storm. Featuring both a multiplayer and story mode, Piggy sees players try to evade the titular monster, who must stop survivors from exiting the level.

FUN FACT

Piggy won three awards at the 8th Annual Bloxy Awards, including Game of the Year, Creator of the Year for developer MiniToon, and the Builderman Award of Excellence.

Players must avoid traps and minions to make it out alive. Certain items and weapons will help you take down Piggy for a while too.

ZOMBIE ATTACK

If you've ever wanted to experience what it's like in a zombie film, this is the game to play! You join a team who have to kill waves of zombies, surviving as long as possible. It's not easy! There are lava zombies, sand zombies and HUGE bosses to take out. When you start with just a pistol you might find it pretty tricky, but soon you'll have access to bigger, more powerful weapons.

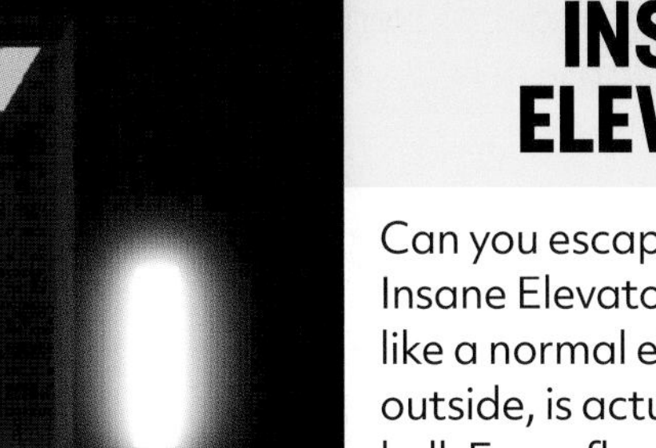

INSANE ELEVATOR

Can you escape the endless Insane Elevator? What looks like a normal elevator from the outside, is actually a trip to hell. Every floor is a nightmare, where killers and monsters rampage the area trying to eliminate you. Players have to do their best to run and hide, staying away from the nasty bad guys.

BANANA EATS

There's a mutant banana on the loose! In Banana Eats, you play a killer game of hide and seek. Taking place over several rounds, you either have to hide from the terrifying banana, or play as the fruit and gobble up as many players as possible. At first, everything feels really funny, but as the time runs out in rounds and the banana starts closing in, it gets super terrifying.

SPOT THE DIFFERENCE

Can you find the seven differences between these action-packed shots from Tower of Hell.

Answers on page 69

ESCAPING HELL

Can you survive the Tower of Hell? See if you can find a route through the tower to make it to the exit.

Answers on page 69

GAME PROFILES

PARKOUR RUN

Think you have perfect timing, reflexes and accuracy? Then obbys might be your strong suit. These crazy courses make you run, hop, skip and jump your way through, over and around obstacles to reach the finish line. Can you make it to the end?

MEGA EASY OBBY

This selection of obby courses is quite easy, as the name suggests, but you'll still find some really cool obstacles that test your parkour and platforming abilities. It's the perfect entry into the genre.

There a lots of different obstacles to have a go at, like giant balls, stars and climbing frames. If you're finding even this a bit too tricky, you can turn on 'easy mode' which removes the 'lava' blocks that send you back to the start of the course.

Along the way, there are jetpacks and other awesome items that, when used, will give you a bit more help on any section causing you trouble. Once you've mastered this obby, it's time to move onto something a little tougher!

FUN FACT

New stages are being added all the time, so check back in often and challenge your friends.

TOWER OF HELL

When we said to try something a bit tougher, we didn't mean THIS tough! It's called Tower of Hell for a reason. Usually an obby has been designed by someone who places each obstacle in a particular place, however, the tower here is randomly generated and always changing.

On top of that, there are no checkpoints to save your progress. Players can spend coins earned in-game to add special effects to each section for a limited time. Trying to jump on a spinning platform while another player makes the whole level foggy is maddening.

You'll get used to what it throws at you if you keep calm and practise your movement skills. After a while, you'll recognise how some platforms move or how you land on smaller blocks. The sense of satisfaction when you have a really good run and get really far is brilliant.

FUN FACT

This is probably the hardest obby on Roblox. Hardly anyone has collected all the badges for this game. Will you get them all?

ALSO TRY

ESCAPE THE HOTEL

SPEED RUN 4

PARKOUR

★ GENRE DEEP-DIVE ★

ROBLOX RANDOMS

There are a lot of bonkers games on Roblox, some of which are very popular. But they're all difficult to categorise as they fly in the face of expectations. It's time to throw genres out the window and look at some games that are a bit on the weird side.

DINOSAUR SIMULATOR

They say life finds a way. The way here, is on Roblox. In Dinosaur Simulator, players choose from a range of different species, big and small, predator or prey. The idea is to live just like the extinct beasts, plodding around to eat, drink and survive. You can explore the prehistoric lands with your dino chums while trying to avoid menaces like the vicious T-rex!

LIFTING SIMULATOR

Starting out as a tiny stickman, this game is about growing muscles and beating up different gods. You start off only able to lift pencils, but as you unlock different weights and increase your strength, you'll end up hefting helicopters! Once you're strong enough, you can take on different enemies and pantheons to earn more money and unlock bigger weights, continuing the cycle.

BUILD A BOAT FOR TREASURE

Players must build a sturdy vessel in order to survive a down-river journey. While that doesn't sound exciting from the offset, danger is always heading in your direction – falling rocks, cannons firing and even geysers that blast your boat into the air on a spout of water. The only way to survive is to build a boat using the strongest materials – you'll get new items with each run!

THE DROPPER

In The Dropper, you have to jump into a pit and dodge objects on the way down. If you reach the bottom, you move on to the next round. However, some of these stages are super difficult, with tiny gaps to squeeze your avatar through. If you happen to hit a snowman, lollipop or whatever else might be in the way ... you explode into pieces! It takes a surprising amount of skill to fall with grace!

RAGDOLL ENGINE

Who doesn't laugh a little when we see someone take a tumble? It's not really a game as such, it's more of a playground in which you watch your avatar falling over. There are stairs to throw yourself down, swimming pools to splat into, even cannons that will launch you across the map. And each time your avatar falls, the body flops all over the place. It's bonkers, but incredibly satisfying.

HIDDEN GEMS

You didn't think that we'd shown you all the gems we'd found, did you? Nope, there are plenty more for us to present, starting with this excellent mix of games that have been slowly gaining in popularity.

FISHING SIMULATOR

You arrive on an idyllic island, and learn everything you need from Rod, one of its inhabitants. Catching fish and trading them is the best way to earn more money and buy better gear – from new poles to boats! Each time you cast your line, bubbles appear when a fish is nibbling the bait. Completing a short minigame will land a random fish of differing rarity into your inventory. You can even select from your best catches to display in an aquarium, letting you show off fish to your friends!

BACKPACKING

There's nothing better than getting out to the countryside and sleeping under the stars, which is exactly what Backpacking is about. This survival sim lets you pick a camping spot and explore the surrounding countryside. You might discover wild animals, or your trip may even become dangerous as tornadoes burst from the sky and you're forced to take shelter. Camping is great on your own, but it's better with friends, so why not buddy up and create a campsite for your pals?

MY RESTAURANT

Managing a restaurant should be a piece of cake. Surely all it takes is a bunch of staff, ordering food, seating customers, dealing with complaints and ... well actually, that's all pretty difficult. My Restaurant puts all these tasks in your hands, even the creation of the building itself! Once you've got everything in place and the customers are flowing through the doors, you'll need to watch closely and upgrade accordingly to become the best eatery in the world.

LOOMIAN LEGACY

In Loomian Legacy, it's up to you to try to save the world and the Loomian species – a cute form of animals that can be traded or used in battle. This game offers a great story, lots of dramatic scenes and a full range of evolving Loomians who all have elemental statuses.

There are plant-, water- and fire-based Loomians, plus many more to adopt, tame and command in combat. Collecting and caring for these cute animals is great fun!

COPS AND ROBBERS

Probably the most popular style of role-play on Roblox features two opposing sides – the cops and the robbers. Whether you want to abide by the law or break it, these games demonstrate the high-octane action that the genre is capable of.

MAD CITY

Everyone has a place in Mad City. It's an exciting world of good and evil, of right and wrong. Your first task is to make a big choice – will you fight for justice and all that is good? Or stray to the dark side and become an agent of chaos?

There are only a few roles here – police, prisoner or hero. The mild-mannered police abide by and enforce the law, while heroes wield superpowers to keep the world under control. If you choose to start as a prisoner, you'll be placed in a cell. Upon escaping, you become a criminal or a villain and must cause as much trouble as you can throughout the city.

FUN FACT

Mad City features over 65 unique vehicles to control, including a UFO!

Mad City is bustling with other players, huge buildings and fast cars. There's never a quiet moment – one minute you can be fighting criminals and the next you're breaking out of prison and speeding round in a stolen car. Each action rewards you with XP and as you progress through levels, you'll be rewarded with cool accessories.

JAILBREAK

Life as a criminal in Jailbreak is tougher than many other games. As you break out of jail, you have nothing but the clothes on your back and must do everything you can to earn money – stealing cars, pulling heists, or randomly discovering stashes of cash. Once you've got some money in your pocket, you can buy cars and weapons; everything you need to pull off bigger crimes and live like a kingpin!

A cop's life is easier by comparison – they start with everything they need to catch the bad guys. All they need to do is hunt for dastardly crooks and stop them by any means. With each criminal stopped, you'll earn money which can be spent on better gear.

FUN FACT

In Jailbreak you can team up with your friends to play together; pulling off big heists and splitting the cash or setting out in a convoy of cars to give chase when the criminals are on the run!

As crimes occur, you'll see a pop-up message telling you who is committing a crime and where, so learning the map is important. It can get chaotic when helicopters fly past and police parachute to the ground through a hail of bullets as criminals try to make a speedy getaway.

ALSO TRY

REDWOOD PRISON

PRISON LIFE

CRIMINALITY

SCENE OF THE CRIME

Can you find the hidden objects in this murder mystery scene? Write the coordinates for each item you spot in the box below.

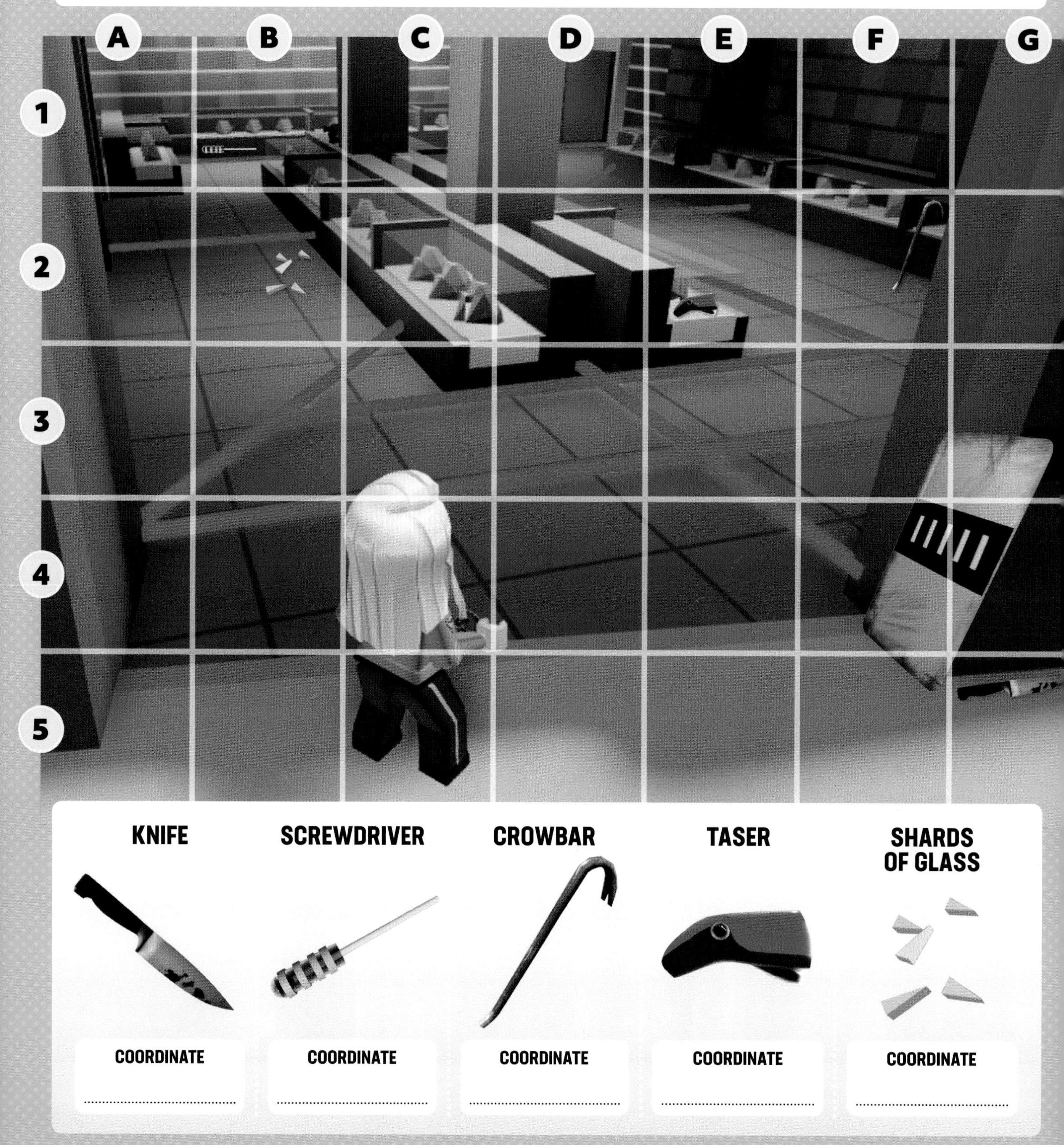

Answers on page 69

MESSY ARMOURY

The guards are trying to respond to an emergency, but someone's made a mess in the armoury. Can you spot how many of each item are in the jumble?

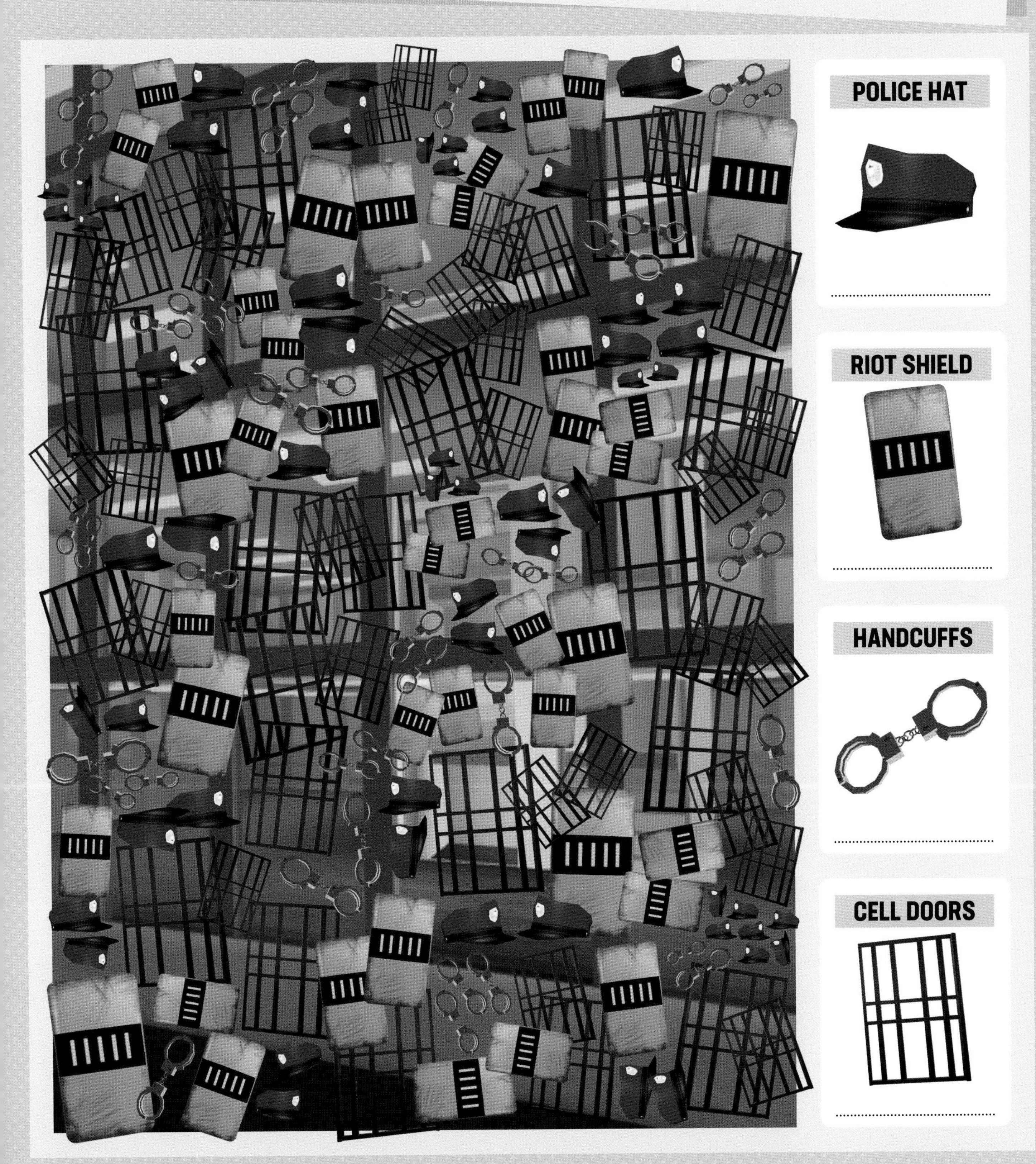

Answers on page 69

★ GENRE DEEP-DIVE ★

SIMULATORS

There's a simulator game for almost everything you can think of. It's easy to check out sims about cars or superpowers, but the truly oddball ideas tend to be a lot of fun. Let's look at a few games that push the boundaries of the simulator genre.

BEE SWARM SIMULATOR

Don't you sometimes wish you could be a bee, tend to flowers, gather pollen and make honey? No? Well bees are cool and honey is tasty, so check out Bee Swarm Simulator to experience life with the buzzy friends.

Head into the fields with your first bee in tow, collect pollen, turn it to honey and use that sweet treat to buy even better bees! Just beware of the monsters and bigger insects in the fields – you can't fight, but your bees will protect you.

FUN FACT

The official Bee Swarm Simulator Club fan group has over eight million fans. But that's nothing compared to the number os visits the game has received – over 1.4 BILLION!

DESTRUCTION SIMULATOR

There's not much to Destruction Simulator and that's perhaps why it's so much fun. The idea is simply to blow up objects using a whole host of carnage-wielding weapons, usually resulting in chaotic outcomes. Everything feels straight out of a cartoon, with chunky graphics and over-the-top destructive tools. The resultant bricks can be sold to fund bigger and better booms.

FUN FACT

There are plenty of buffs to apply to your pets when you complete tasks or discover secrets. These can range from double damage in battles to extra gems as rewards.

SABER SIMULATOR

Swinging your saber builds strength, allowing you to fight ever-bigger bosses and other players. Once your sword has gained enough power, you can sell it for cash and start the process again! You can spend your coins on new sabers and skills in the hopes of being good enough to win the PvP. Swing that sword, get those gains!

TOP TYCOONS

There's something fascinating about growth in games, whether it's physically increasing the size of your character, nurturing an empire or just watching your money stack up. Tycoons capitalise on that addictiveness to create games that will keep you coming back for more.

THEME PARK TYCOON 2

In Theme Park Tycoon 2, you can create a rollercoaster that has too many loops. You can make rides which, in real life, would probably make you vomit. Players can work together to build huge attractions that defy the laws of physics.

FUN FACT

Each server can hold up to six players, with everyone able to work on one park together. Why not create a family theme park as a joint project?

As well as rollercoasters, there are all your usual rides – the teacups, the swinging ship and even a log flume. It's up to you to build a great park people want to visit. But it's not just about fun – make sure there are food places and loos!

With these things in place, not only will you have a successful park, you can take some time out to ride the attractions yourself. With lots of different types of scenery to choose from, you can give your park a theme, or break it down into zones.

TROPICAL RESORT TYCOON

Creating the perfect holiday resort seems like an easy task – plenty of comfy rooms, a large swimming pool and lots of good food. But getting it all to fit on your own personal island, while keeping everyone entertained, isn't always simple.

FUN FACT

Only a handful of people have unlocked this game's toughest badge, to earn over a billion in currency.

Thankfully, in between building hotels and furnishing rooms, you can take out a sports car or speedboat and explore your paradise. Invite friends to come and stay, see what they think of your resort and change things up once they leave.

You earn money from each visitor, which you can use to upgrade rooms and services, attracting more customers to your hotel and making it the best resort in the world! You'll need a holiday after all that work though ...

ALSO TRY

LUMBER TYCOON 2

CAR DEALERSHIP TYCOON

SPACE COMBAT TYCOON

RTHRO

Over the months since Rthro avatars were released, many more games have started to incorporate the new design. Sometimes it can be difficult to adapt to change, so, we've picked some great games that will help you fully get into the Rthro style!

GIANT SIMULATOR

Growing up can be a pain – it seems to take forever! Luckily in Giant Simulator, it's a matter of clicking and collecting. The more time you put in, the bigger you'll be. As you grow, you'll become much stronger and can visit dungeons to look for treasure and fight random monsters, or other players, along the way. The growth mechanic is great for highlighting the Rthro changes as you get bigger and bigger.

FUN FACT

Rthro avatars first came to Roblox in October 2018, and aimed to give players more human-like characteristics. It didn't replace the previous R6 and R15 models though!

BAD BUSINESS

If you're looking for a great shooter, load up Bad Business. There's a lot to enjoy here, with realistic weapons, great movement and plenty of interesting maps. There are plenty of rewards as you level up and an option to select a loadout of weapons that suit your playstyle. It's mostly team-based, and while the view is in first-person, Rthro is utilised well to show your different body parts and other players.

LEGENDS OF SPEED

There's something very exciting about being able to run fast. Legends of Speed is all about building up your pace until you're as fast as lightning. As you work your way through the gears, you'll face off with plenty of other people in races, where you can win or pick up gems. These can be exchanged for pets or light trails that burst from your feet. And because the game is in the Rthro style, the running animations look awesome!

SUPER STRIKER LEAGUE

The Rthro changes make Roblox avatars look much more human, with more joints and sections to the skeleton. This means sports games not only play better but look better too. Super Striker League sets up 3v3 football matches on an enclosed pitch, which means no corner kicks or throw-ins. Teams try to score as many goals as possible in five minutes, taking control of a fully customisable player and utilising flashy power-ups.

★ GENRE DEEP-DIVE ★

TOWER DEFENCE

If waves of enemies are storming towards you, it's sometimes a good idea to defend rather than attack. In these tower defence games, you'll decide the placement of powerful towers that will defend your base from an onslaught of invaders. Do you have the wits to keep it safe?

TOWER DEFENCE SIMULATOR

Entering any of the maps in Tower Defence Simulator makes you appear as a giant, overseeing a map of criss-crossing paths in the arena. At one end, your precious base, at the other, a doorway where zombies will emerge. Thankfully, these are polite zombies that stick to the route, meaning you can place defending units at tactical spots for maximum damage. But they'll keep coming, in greater numbers and often more powerful variants in every wave.

FUN FACT

The game often welcomes seasonal bosses, like Krampus and Ducky DOOM. They reward a badge when you defeat them, but are only available for a limited

ALL STAR TOWER DEFENCE

In All Star Tower Defence you have the opportunity to place the greatest anime heroes. In all of these tower defence games, once a unit is placed, it's possible to upgrade them by clicking them and investing more money. This makes your army tougher and more able to hold back the waves of foes. Beware, any enemies that make it past your defence will slowly erode the energy bar of your base – once that hits zero, it's game over.

FUN FACT

ASTD features heroes from popular shows like Fairy Tale, Dragonball Z, One Piece and Naruto.

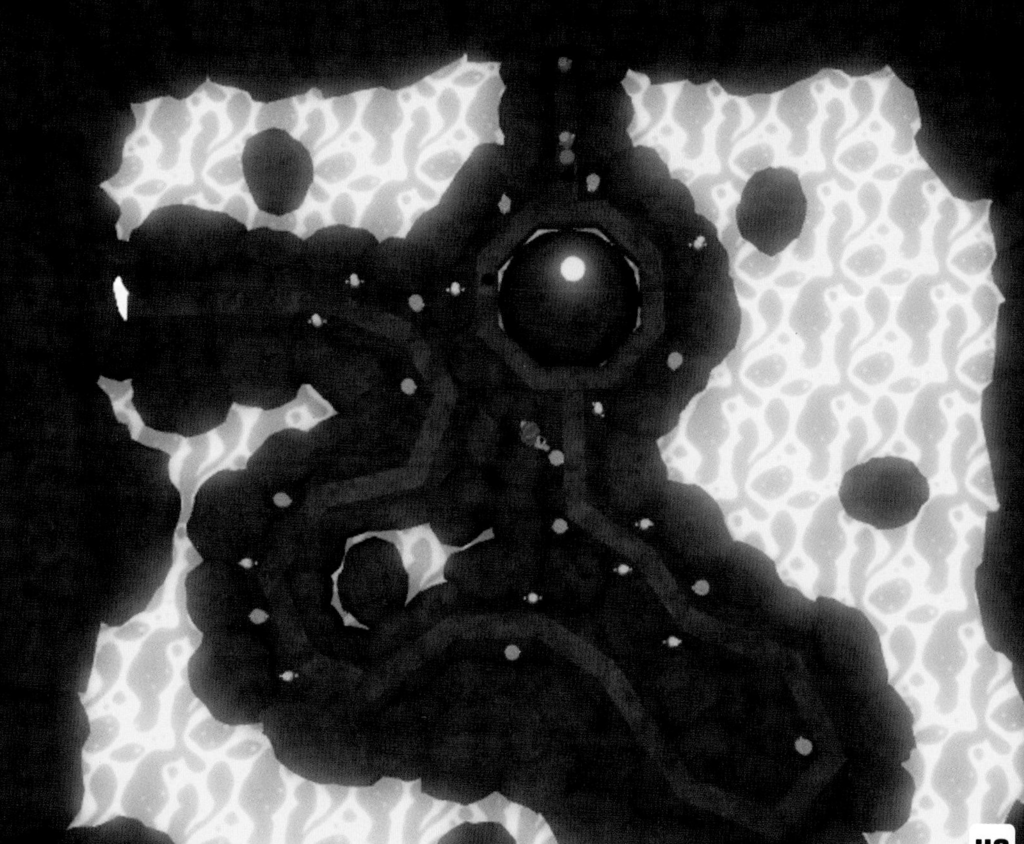

TOWER HEROES

Things become more fantastical in Tower Heroes, with wizards and warriors battling in an otherworldly realm. Each unit costs some of your currency and there's a limit to the number of units you can place. The balance comes from which units you choose, where you place them and how they attack. The units will battle any enemies that enter their attack radius, generating coins that can be used to unlock and upgrade even more powerful heroes.

HIGH FANTASY

Sometimes you just need to take a break from the real world, which is why the fantasy genre has always been so popular. These games are filled with exotic locations, mysterious folk and quests that can transport you all around strange realms.

CREATURES OF SONARIA

If simply owning a pet is starting to becoming a little boring, then Creatures of Sonaria may be the game for you. You become one of the fantastical creatures, like the flying Brequewk, and must try to survive and become an adult.

To reach adulthood, you'll need to take care of your stats, whether that's drinking water, making sure you've got a full belly, or avoiding being killed by predators. Different creatures eat different foods, so while some will happily munch plants, others prefer to eat creatures ...

You can buddy up with other players to create an imaginative clan of monsters. You can hunt in a pack, or make use of everyone's strengths to ensure you can survive for as long as possible.

DUNGEON QUEST

Dungeon-crawling is a very popular part of many role-playing games. Dungeon Quest kicks it up a notch and uses this concept as the central point of the game. By fighting and completing each dungeon, your avatar will find loads of awesome equipment, items and weapons to use in the next adventure, making them stronger with every run.

Traditionally these dungeon-crawlers hand out loot randomly and that's certainly the case here. You might not always get exactly what you're looking for but that's part of the fun and why players keep grinding through dungeons.

Players gather together to take on larger fights or harder dungeons and tend to slot into roles which fit their playstyle; ranged DPS plays at distance keeping up a high level of damage, a tank will absorb hits protecting those around them, melee DPS gets up close and handles most of the fighting with high power moves. Finally, a healer cares for all, keeping their health up and preventing a team wipe.

FUN FACT

Dungeon Quest was considered by many players and designers as the best game of 2019 and it's still going strong.

FUN FACT

There are eight dungeons in the game currently – Desert Temple, Winter Outpost, Pirate Island, King's Castle, Underworld, Samurai Palace, The Canals and Ghastly Harbor.

ALSO TRY

A UNIVERSAL TIME

WORLD // ZERO

ALL STAR TOWER DEFENCE

Build your theme park empire by finding the correct slot for these six pieces to complete the scene.

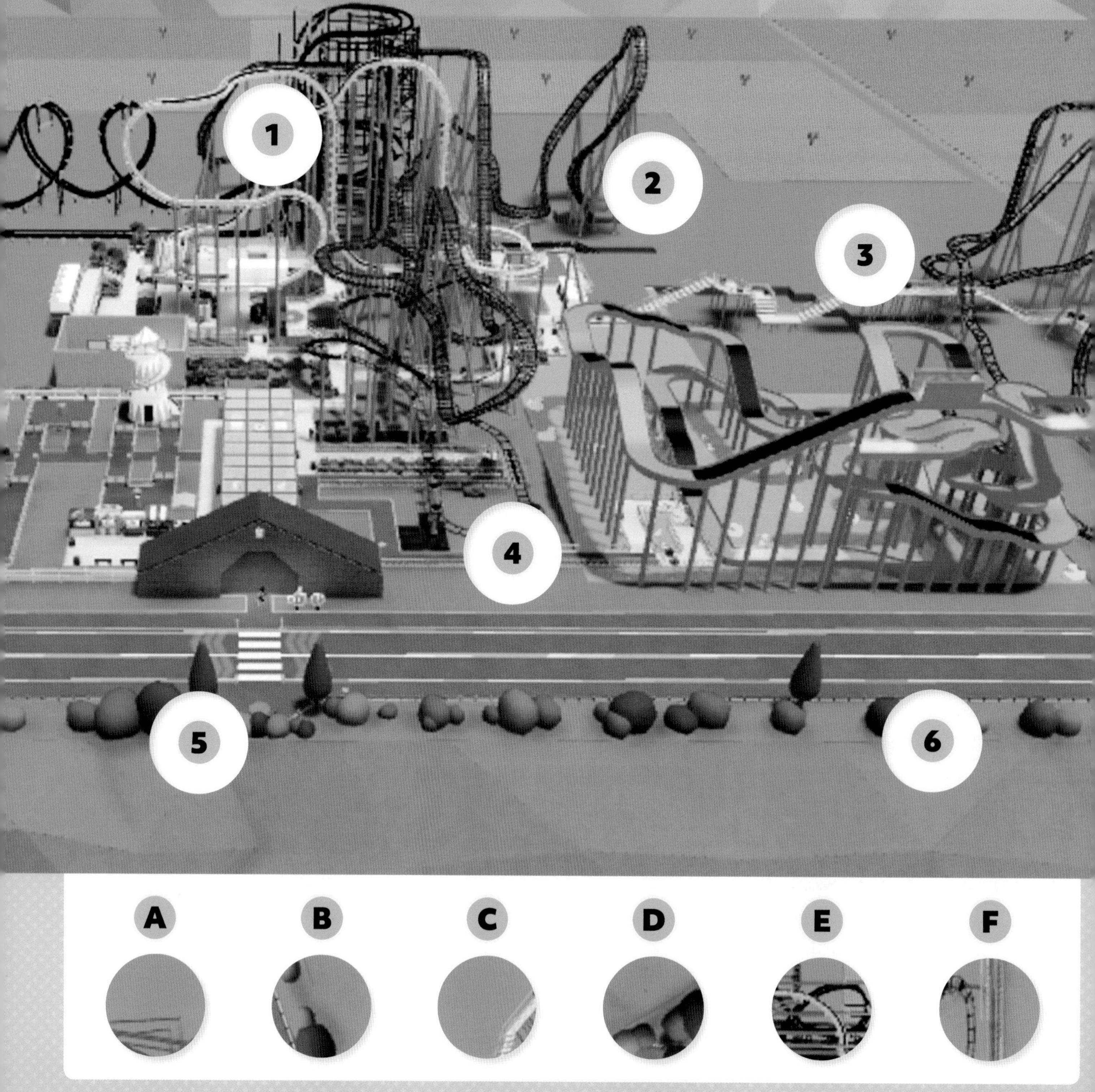

Answers on page 69

FRUITY FOE

The banana is on the loose! Follow the paths from the killer banana to see which avatars it catches and which one escapes!

A

B

C

D

Answers on page 69

★ GENRE DEEP-DIVE ★

EDUCATIONAL

Among the more popular, more adrenaline-fuelled games, there are some that transport you to a world of learning. Interactive games are becoming more common in schools for a broad range of subjects. The beauty of Roblox is that you can find many of these games here.

EXPEDITION ANTARCTICA

This is an opportunity to walk in the footsteps of great explorers. Starting from expedition HQ, you must equip proper safety gear – helmet, thermal coat, backpack – before you head out to the icy tundra on the way to the South Pole. You'll need to navigate difficult terrain using ladders and ropes as you move from ice patches to icebergs. Of course, along the way you'll see some of the native wildlife, as well as others on their own expedition.

FUN FACT

Among the penguins of the South Pole, there's one that's wearing a backpack. If you can find it and click on it, you'll receive a gift ...

ROBLOX TITANIC

Most people are aware of the sinking of the Titanic in 1912, which occurred after it struck an iceberg in one of the greatest tragedies in history. Roblox Titanic gives you a chance to step into the shoes of a passenger exploring the ship, which has been replicated in great detail. Then water begins to rush into the ship and you must attempt to survive, by walking similar paths to those who were on board.

ROCKET TESTER

With over 50 rockets, all based on historic launches, you have the opportunity to see, explore and launch crafts yourself. You can spawn any spacefaring vehicles on a launch pad, and watch it blast off from expertly recreated space stations, or even ride certain craft to other planets and moons. Rocket Tester offers great information for each rocket, so you can learn all about the country of origin, the mission in which it was launched and how well it fared.

FUN FACT

Take a break from launching rockets to build your own space station on the surface of moons and planets. You can use them as base camps for further exploration.

SHOOT 'EM UPS

There's no better test of skill, reflexes and temperament than a shooting game. Whether you're going solo in a free-for-all or rallying your squad in a team deathmatch, these iconic games have a habit of separating the noobs from the masters.

FUN FACT

Arsenal has won THREE Bloxy awards in the past, for Best Sound, Best Trailer and Game of the Year.

ARSENAL

Arsenal is a very different type of shooter, one that structures itself to be as random as possible and gets harder as the round goes on. The standard format is the first to 32 kills, but the twist comes as you reach the 30 kills, when you're forced to use the golden gun.

The golden gun is an instant kill if it hits the opponent, but requires more precision. When you've made a kill with golden gun, you'll have to achieve the final kill with a golden knife, which requires getting up close and personal. Both make the end of a match really tense.

FUN FACT

If you have the 'delivery' badge from Work at a Pizza Place, you'll unlock the exclusive pizza boy skin in Arsenal.

With each death and round change, you're given a random gun, which might mean you end up with weapons you dislike. Arsenal embraces seasonal content, often changing the game entirely for Halloween or Christmas, so it's worth checking in often.

BIG PAINTBALL

Shooters don't need to be realistic and gritty. BIG Paintball throws you into bright and colourful arena to trade paintballs. But don't let the brightness fool you, it still requires a lot of skill and practice to succeed.

Playing as part of a team, you can adopt one of many playstyles. An average match will have sharpshooters hanging back with snipers, while gunners run up front and lay down covering fire.

It's a great combo of smart shooter and arcade-style visuals that makes it suitable for players of all ages. Who doesn't enjoy splatting paintballs at an enemy?

ALSO TRY

BLACKHAWK RESCUE MISSION 5

ENTRY POINT

WAR SIMULATOR

HIDDEN GEMS

The final segment of our spotlight on lesser-known games has everything from sick skating to vehicular mayhem! With all these excellent games at your disposal, you'll have plenty of games ready to wow your friends with.

CAR CRUSHERS 2

Destruction simulators are great when you want to let off some steam. In Car Crushers 2, you do exactly as the title suggests; grab a car and destroy it. You can crush it, slice it, plunge it into a pit full of whirling blades or just drive it down a staircase. Whichever you choose, the car will shatter into pieces, rewarding you with money and spare parts, used to unlock better machines of destruction, and more vehicles to destroy.

SKATE PARK

Worried you might injure yourself on a real skateboard? Not to worry, head over to Skate Park and bust out your board for some sick tricks. There are no insane button combos; just press a certain button. Even if you don't know the difference between a kickflip and an ollie, you can have great fun zooming round half pipes and kickers pulling off awesome sets.

WORD BOMB

Players gather around a ticking bomb and must type words based on a prompt. If you don't choose a word fast enough, the bomb blows up and you lose a bit of health. For example, you may be given the prompt "type a word with 'OM' in it" and could answer with 'BOMB'. It's a great game for practising your typing speed and testing your vocab.

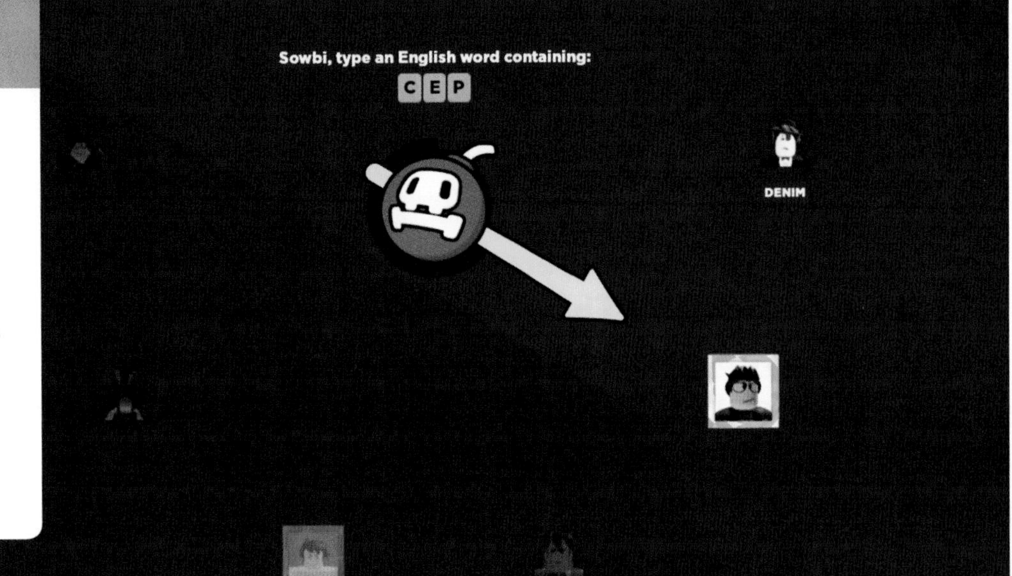

CRUISE [STORY]

A happy, colourful cruise ship where you and you friends, can gather to play minigames. Join Captain Jack for a voyage on the wide open ocean for lots of fun.

Choose a cabin to stay in, dance to cool music and even fight boarding piartes. It's all fun and games on this cruise ship – just don't spend all your cruise bucks on the buffet!

PLAYER V PLAYER

PvP, or 'player versus player', focuses on competition over cooperation. There are thousands of games that pit players against each other, but each offers something unique, whether you want to become the best, or just mess around with mates.

VEHICLE SIMULATOR

If racing is your thing, Vehicle Simulator has every type of transport you can imagine. And all of them can be raced either via the in-game official races or just with you and some friends arranging your own burnout.

There are chase races, where one car must catch another to win, as well as obstacles such as loops and corkscrews. If you don't fancy four wheels, choose a plane or helicopter instead!

FUN FACT

Simbuilder, the developer of Vehicle Simulator has also worked on Turbo Havoc, which is a car-meets-football game inspired by the smash-hit *Rocket League*.

ASSASSIN!

A battle royale with a difference, Assassin! puts a handful of players on a map in order to crown one winner. Where it differs from others is in how you deal with opponents. At the start of the round and on each kill, you are told to hunt a specific player while a sole player hunts you. This makes it a race to find your target and take them out before you're eliminated.

HIDE AND SEEK EXTREME

Everyone has played Hide and Seek at some point in their life so you should know the drill: one person is the seeker and must find everyone hiding. What makes this version extreme is the world in which you play – as shrunken people in the normal world. One time you might be playing in a games room filled with giant pool tables and the next, in a kitchen where the oven is as big as a house!

SUPER DOOMSPIRE

In Super Doomspire, the idea is to stop your enemy from spawning into the game by blowing up their base. Everyone starts with a big building in which they spawn when they die, but if the building isn't there, they can't spawn and can't win. It's a simple and addictive game that is full of laughs. Using bombs, rocket launchers (and swords for enemy players) your task it to completely destroy the opposing team's base.

MYSTERIOUS

Some games are obvious and straightforward, others ... not so much. If you prefer a game that challenges your brain as well as your reflexes, then this pair of games might be of particular interest to you. Elementary, dear reader.

MURDER MYSTERY 2

Can you work out a mystery based on the movements of other players? 12 players enter a map – ten innocent bystanders, a sheriff and a murderer. Depending on who you become when you spawn in, you'll have a specific task.

As an innocent, you simply need to survive by hiding; the sheriff must protect the innocent players with their gun; while the killer tries to murder as many people as possible, without being caught.

The twist? The sheriff can also be killed, leaving their gun behind. Anyone who collects this becomes a hero and takes on the role of protector. Once the time runs out, will you win as an uncaught killer? Or catch the murderer as they try to wipe out the innocents?

IMPOSTOR

Similar to Murder Mystery 2; the idea here is to find a hidden impostor among an innocent party. However, this impostor is trying their best to kill ALL innocent players before they're caught. By sabotaging a mission, they infiltrate the player group and wander a map seeking out unwitting players going about their tasks.

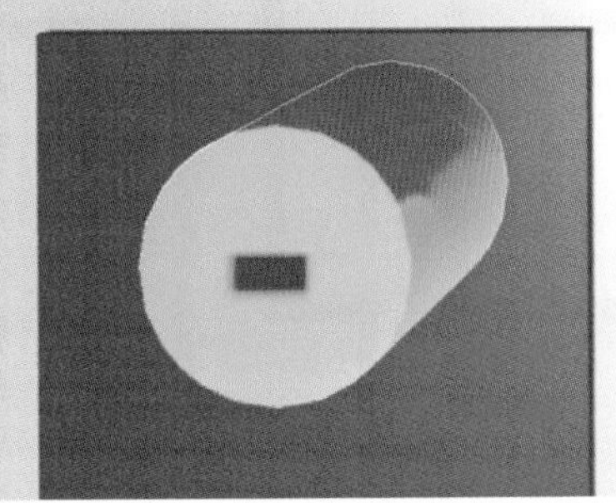

Once the impostor strikes and eliminates a player, it's up to the surviving innocents to work out who the impostor is by discussing the movements of each player, how they act, where they were and whether they were acting suspiciously.

At the end of the discussion, it's up to everyone to vote who they think the impostor is and boot them off the map. Identify the impostor correctly and you win. Play as the impostor and survive accusations of the innocent players and you'll win instead.

ALSO TRY

FLICKER

OUTLASTER

HUNTED

WOOD FOR THE TREES

The lumberjack has found a forest to chop through, but left his axe back at home. Can you help him find a way out so he can collect it?

Answers on page 69

AFTER DARK

They say the city never sleeps and these five busy folks are up and about very late. Can you match each avatar to its shadow?

NINJA

2

1

FAIRY

3

RACING DRIVER

WEIGHTLIFTER

5

4

CHEF

Answers on page 69

GOODBYE!

What a trip this has been!

Phew! Together we've travelled through so much of Roblox; old and new worlds unfolded in front of us. We've played on our own and with friends – maybe you even made a few new ones along the way.

By now you must have seen every game we discussed, possibly some we didn't, and hopefully gave them all a try. Perhaps you found a new favourite game that you can't wait to talk more about?

Roblox is a world of creativity, big and small. There's space for everything and everyone. Nobody gets left out. There are some oddball games, some serious contenders and those that will just never stop growing.

Maybe you have an idea you'd like to create one day and are thinking about Roblox for its home. With billions of players, there's always someone who will play along.

Above all, we hope you had fun and will continue to enjoy every moment in Roblox safely. Work together with others, treat them how you'd like to be treated and remember, games are meant to be fun.

We'll see you next time!

SALOON

STAYING SAFE ONLINE

YOUNGER FANS' GUIDE

Spending time online is great fun. These games might be your first experience of digital socialising, so here are a few simple rules to help you stay safe and keep the internet an awesome place to spend time:

- Never give out your real name – don't use it as your username.
- Never give out any of your personal details.
- Never tell anybody which school you go to or how old you are.
- Never tell anybody your password, except a parent or guardian.
- Before registering for any account, ask a parent or guardian for permission.
- Take regular breaks, as well as playing with parents nearby, or in shared family rooms.
- Always tell a parent or guardian if something is worrying you.

PARENTS' GUIDE

ONLINE CHAT

In most games, there is live on-screen text chat between users. Parents are advised to ensure that their children are only talking to friends and that they aren't being exposed to any adult matter.

SOUND

Sound is crucial in many video games. Players will often wear headphones, meaning parents won't be able to hear what children are listening to. Set up your console or computer to have sound coming from the TV or monitor as well as the headset so you can hear what your child is experiencing.

REPORTING PLAYERS

If you see or hear a player being abusive, Roblox allows you to report users or interactions. You'll be able to use the Report Abuse links found throughout the site on game pages, but there may also be buttons within chat windows or game menus where you can raise a case with community managers.

SCREEN TIME

Taking regular breaks is important. Set play sessions by using a timer. Some games can last a long time and if your child finishes playing in the middle of a round, they could leave their teammates a person short and lose any points they've earned. It is advisable to give an advanced warning for stopping play or clearly outlining a stopping point before play begins.

IN-GAME PURCHASES

Many games offer in-app purchases to enhance the game experience but they're not required to play the game. They also don't improve a player's performance. There are ways to set up safety measures on you child's account by setting up a PIN through Settings. Consult these before allowing your child to play any game in order to avoid any unpermitted spending on your account.

ANSWERS

Check your answers here!

Page 12 – City Walk

Page 13 – MeepCity Sudoku

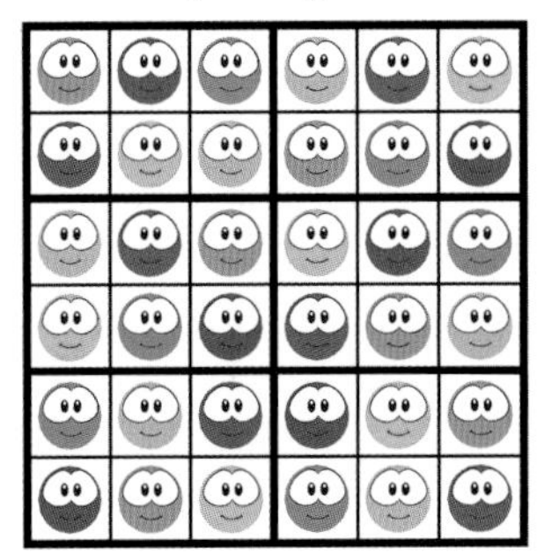

Page 20 – Animal Jumbles
1 - Unicorn, 2 - Giraffe, 3 - Griffin, 4 - Panda, 5 - Turtle, 6 - Kangaroo

Page 21 – Pet Pairs
Dog - bone, Dragon - pile of gold, Horse - hay bale, Bee - honeycomb, Cat - ball of yarn

Page 30 – Spot the Difference

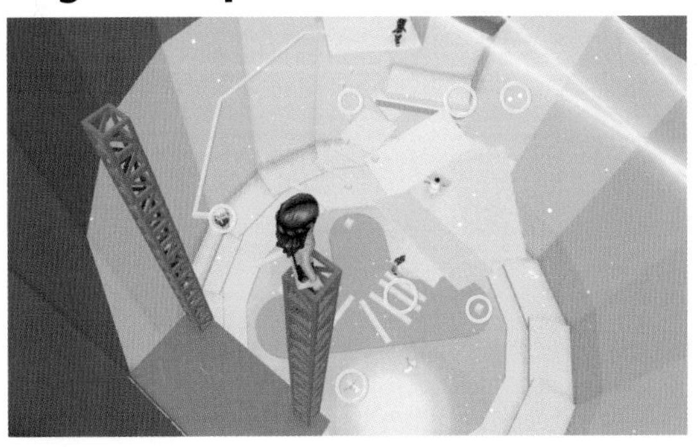

Page 31 – Escaping Hell

Page 40 – Scene of the Crime
Knife - G5, Screwdriver - B1, Crowbar - F2, Taser - E2, Shards of glass - B2

Page 41 – Messy Armoury
Police hat - 59, Riot shield - 39, Handcuffs - 39, Cell doors - 48

Page 52 – Master Tycoon
A - 2, B - 6, C - 3, D - 5, E - 1, F - 4

Page 53 – Fruity Foe
The avatar that escapes is C

Page 64 – Wood for the Trees

Page 65 – After Dark
Fairy - 4, Ninja - 5, Racing driver - 1, Weightlifter - 2, Chef - 3